ASSASSIN'S
CREED® IV
BLACK FLAG™

THE ART OF ASSASSIN'S CREED® IV: BLACK FLAG™

Published by Titan Books
A division of Titan Publishing Group Ltd.
144 Southwark St.
London SE1 0UP

First edition: October 2013

10 9 8 7 6 5 4 3 2 1

To receive advance information, news, competitions, and exclusive offers online, please sign up for the Titan newsletter on our website: www.titanbooks.com

A CIP catalogue record for this title is available from the British Library.
ISBN: 9781783290239

Printed and bound in United Arab Emirates.

CONTENTS

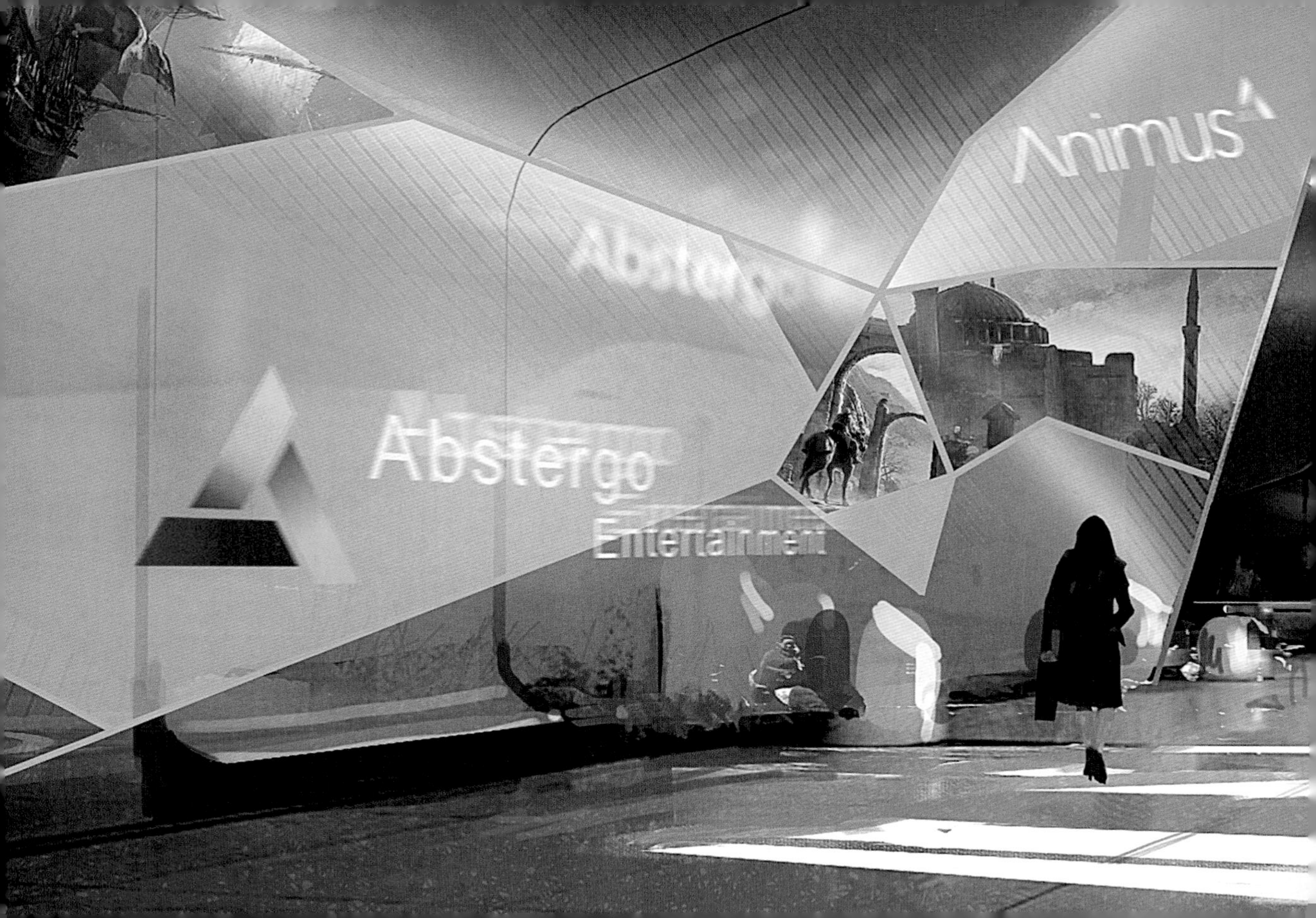
Animus
Abstergo
Entertainment

7H65AN-B88

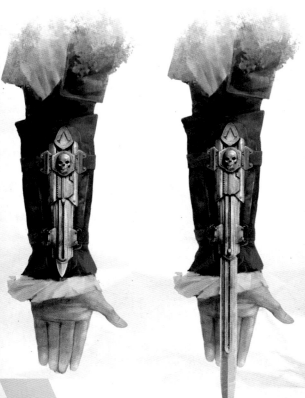

15

16

6

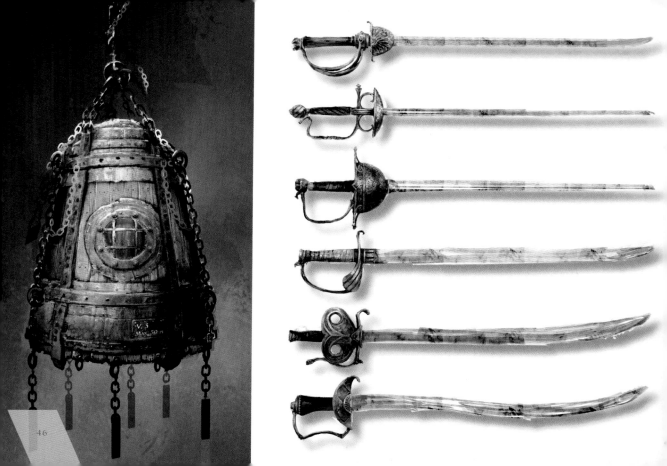

SHIPS

7

Front

Side

53

54

Front View

Bow 船首

1st Rate   3rd Rate   Aquila   Brig   Schooner   Sloop   ROWBOAT!

8

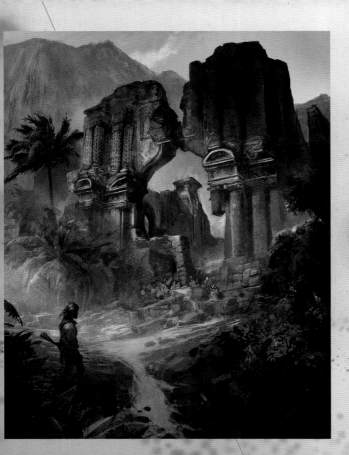

CREDITS

STUDIO – MONTREAL

Martin Deschambault I *Artist*
Maxime Desmettre I *Artist*
Vincent Gaigneux I *Artist*
Patrick Lambert I *Artist*
Donglu Yu I *Artist*
Raphael Lacoste I *Brand Art Director*

STUDIO – SINGAPORE

Max Qin I *Artist*
Kobe Sek I *Artist*
Guang Yu Tan I *Artist*
Lixiong Tan I *Artist*
Yong Jin Teo I *Artist*
Jing-Cherng Wong I *Artist*

STUDIO – SOFIA

Eddie Bennun I *Artist*
Ivan Koritarev I *Artist*

UBISOFT – BRAND

Sebastien Puel I *Executive Producer*
Julien Cuny I *Brand Content Director*
Etienne Allonier I *Brand Director*
Aymar Azaizia I *Brand Project Manager*
Antoine Ceszynski I *Brand Product Manager*

UBISOFT – US

Laurent Detoc, President I *North America*
Tony Key I *SVP, Sales and Marketing*
Adam Novickas I *Sr. Director, Marketing*
Danny Ruiz I *Director, Marketing*
Lindsay Cohen I *Sr. Brand Manager*
Tina Chan I *Brand Manager*
Joogy Park I *Brand Manager*
Katrina Medema I *Purchasing Manager*
Christine Chin I *Purchasing Coordinator*
Scranton Stichal I *Assistant Buyer*
Emmy Lee I *Key Master*

UBISOFT – EMEA

Alain Corre I *EMEA Executive Director*
Geoffroy Sardin I *EMEA Chief Marketing Sales Officer*
Guillaume Carmona I *EMEA Brand Director*
Julien Delalande I *EMEA Group Brand Manager*
Gwenn Berhault I *EMEA Senior Brand Manager*
Damien Guillotin I *EMEA Brand Manager*
Louis Perrazi I *EMEA Brand Manager Assistant*
Dorian Kirschstetter I *EMEA Brand Manager Assistant*

UBISOFT – MARKETING

Carsten Myhill I *Brand Manager*
Thomas Moreau I *Product Manager*
David Bedard I *Product Manager*
Nicolas Lefebvre I *Product Manager*